POINTS OF VIEW

Do Kids Need RECESS?

By Amy B. Rogers

KidHaven PUBLISHING

Published in 2019 by
KidHaven Publishing, an Imprint of Greenhaven Publishing, LLC
353 3rd Avenue
Suite 255
New York, NY 10010

Designer: Deanna Paternostro
Editor: Katie Kawa

Photo credits: Cover TinnaPong/Shutterstock.com; p. 5 (top) Patrick Foto/Shutterstock.com; p. 5 (bottom) Iakov Filimonov/Shutterstock.com; p. 7 (top-left) Matt Clayton/View Pictures/UIG via Getty Images; p. 7 (top-right) Mohamad ESLAMI RAD/Gamma-Rapho via Getty Images; p. 7 (bottom-left) Christer Fredriksson/Lonely Planet Images/Getty Images; p. 7 (bottom-right) Westend61/Westend61/Getty Images; p. 9 (top) Santhosh Varghese/Shutterstock.com; pp. 9 (bottom), 15, 21 (inset, right) wavebreakmedia/Shutterstock.com; p. 11 Syda Productions/Shutterstock.com; p. 13 2xSamara.com/Shutterstock.com; p. 17 Hurst Photo/Shutterstock.com; p. 19 Monkey Business Images/Shutterstock.com; p. 21 (notepad and inset, middle-left) ESB Professional/Shutterstock.com; p. 21 (markers) Kucher Serhii/Shutterstock.com; p. 21 (photo frame) FARBAI/iStock/Thinkstock; p. 21 (inset, left) karelnoppe/Shutterstock.com; p. 21 (inset, middle-right) Happy Together/Shutterstock.com

Cataloging-in-Publication Data

Names: Rogers, Amy B.
Title: Do kids need recess? / Amy B. Rogers.
Description: New York : KidHaven Publishing, 2019. | Series: Points of view | Includes glossary and index.
Identifiers: ISBN 9781534527850 (pbk.) | ISBN 9781534527874 (library bound) | ISBN 9781534527867 (6 pack) | ISBN 9781534527881 (ebook)
Subjects: LCSH: School recess breaks–Juvenile literature. | Play–Juvenile literature. | Physical education and training–Juvenile literature.
Classification: LCC LB3033.R64 2019 | DDC 371.2'42–dc23

Printed in the United States of America

CPSIA compliance information: Batch #BW19KL: For further information contact Greenhaven Publishing LLC, New York, New York at 1-844-317-7404.

Please visit our website, www.greenhavenpublishing.com. For a free color catalog of all our high-quality books, call toll free 1-844-317-7404 or fax 1-844-317-7405.

CONTENTS

Playtime Points OF VIEW

What's your favorite part of the school day? Some students like math class, while others like music. For many students, one of the best parts of the day is recess. They like having free time to play on their own or with their friends.

Recess is fun, and many people believe it's important for kids, too. However, other people believe it's not as important as learning facts and preparing for tests. These people sometimes make decisions that lead to recess being cut from the school day. Do you think kids need recess? Read on to learn facts you can use to support your point of view!

Know the Facts!

A major study of recess in the United States was done in 2016. This study showed that eight states required elementary schools to give students time for recess every day.

It's easy to say that kids need recess because it's fun. However, that's not an informed, or educated, opinion. An informed opinion is supported by facts.

Recess Around the WORLD

Recess is a part of the school day for students around the world. Although the games they play might be different, some things are generally the same. Many schools around the world have recess around lunchtime, and recess activities in many countries take place outside when possible.

Different countries provide students with different amounts of time for recess. For example, the average amount of time for recess in U.S. schools is around 27 minutes each day. However, students in Finland and Japan take breaks for 10 to 15 minutes each hour.

Know the Facts!

Students in China are given exercise breaks during the school day. This includes a break for eye exercises!

Schoolyards around the world are filled with the sounds of kids playing every day at recess.

Helping STUDENTS

Although recess generally takes place outside the classroom, it plays a part in what happens in the classroom, too. Even one recess break each day has been shown to improve student achievement, which is measured by classroom grades and test scores. **Experts** believe **physical** activity, which students get during recess, improves memory and **focus**, which helps students do well in class.

Recess also helps improve classroom behavior, which is how students act in the classroom. Studies have shown that students who don't get time for recess every day have a harder time paying attention and sitting still in class.

Know the Facts!

Recess is sometimes taken away from students as a **punishment**. However, in 2013, a group of U.S. doctors who deal with children said that recess shouldn't be taken away from children for any reason, including bad classroom behavior.

Many people believe kids need recess because they don't have long attention spans. This means they can't focus on one task for a long time. They need breaks to give their minds a rest so they can then focus on the next task.

Testing Takes TIME

Recess can help students do well on tests, but many people believe it's not as much help as more time in the classroom. These people believe students need extra time for math, reading, and other classes much more than they need recess.

In recent years, U.S. students have started taking more standardized tests. These are tests that are taken and graded in a consistent way to allow people to compare students' achievements by looking at their test scores. As these tests have become more important, some schools have taken away recess to give teachers more time for test preparation.

Know the Facts!

U.S. students generally spend 20 to 25 hours each year taking standardized tests. By the time they finish high school, they've taken an average of 112 standardized tests!

Standardized tests are a major part of life for U.S. students today. Other parts of the school day, such as art classes, music classes, and recess, are sometimes cut to give students more time to prepare for these tests.

Healthy KIDS

People who believe students need recess argue that it's good for a child's body as well as their grades. Recess gives students time during the school day to be physically active, which is an important part of staying healthy.

Doctors have stated that children should get at least 1 hour of physical activity every day. This can help fight childhood **obesity**, which is a major problem in the United States. Playing during recess is a fun way to stay physically fit, and doctors believe it's good for students' **mental** health, too.

Know the Facts!

Experts have said that all students should be given at least 20 minutes for recess every day.

Doctors have stated that the physical activity kids take part in during recess is good for their **muscles**, bones, heart, brain, and many other body parts.

Already ACTIVE

Most people agree that it's important for kids to be physically active. However, some people argue that kids already have a part of their school day that was created for physical activity. These people believe that physical education classes—also known as PE or gym—give students enough time to be active outside the classroom.

Many kids play sports, take dance lessons, or do other physical activities after school, too. Some people believe these activities can be used instead of recess to help kids get moving without taking up time at school.

Know the Facts!

A 2017 study showed that about 37 percent of American kids play team sports.

Most students are required to take physical education classes. Some people argue that these classes do enough to get kids moving, so they don't need extra time for recess.

The Importance OF PLAY

Physical education classes and recess keep kids active, but they do this in very different ways. Physical education classes generally follow a plan and make students take part in an **organized** activity together. Recess gives kids more freedom to play on their own and to play by their own rules.

The importance of play is a big reason why people strongly support recess. Having time to play has been shown to improve many parts of kids' lives. Doctors believe it helps them make friends, become more creative, and deal with their feelings in healthy ways.

Know the Facts!

The United Nations—a group that fights for human rights around the world—has stated that the right to play is a basic right for all children.

Many kids are often too busy to play when they get home from school. Recess gives them time every day to have fun with their friends.

Too Much FREEDOM?

Some people believe there's a time and a place for play, and it's not at school. These people argue that kids have plenty of time to play at home, so time at school should be spent learning.

People also argue that recess doesn't always help kids make friends. They worry it can lead to bullying. They also worry that giving kids too much freedom at recess can cause them to get hurt or hurt each other. Kids can also feel left out if they're not asked to take part in activities with their classmates during recess.

Know the Facts!

As of 2016, more than 20 percent of U.S. students have said they've been bullied.

Some people believe the freedom students often have at recess is good for them, but others believe it can lead to bullying.

More Than Just

A DEBATE

The **debate** over the importance of recess has real **consequences** for students. The opinions of people in charge of schools **affect** the decisions they make about how students should spend their day. This is why it's important for all points of view on an issue to be heard. People in charge should know all the facts and the opinions on both sides before they make a decision.

After learning more about these facts and opinions, what do you think? Do kids need recess, or should they spend more time in class learning and preparing for important tests?

Know the Facts!

Studies have shown that kids eat more fruits and vegetables when they have recess before eating lunch.

Do kids need recess?

YES

- Recess helps kids get better grades and have better classroom behavior.
- Kids need to be active every day to stay healthy, and recess gives them a set time each day to be active.
- Recess gives kids free time to play, which helps them in many ways.
- Recess helps kids make friends.

NO

- Recess wastes time that should be used to prepare for standardized tests.
- Recess is not the only time during the school day when kids can be active.
- Time at school should be spent learning because kids can play outside of school.
- Recess can be a time when kids bully each other.

A chart such as this one can be used to break down the main arguments on both sides of an issue such as the importance of recess.

GLOSSARY

affect: To produce an effect on something.

consequence: Something important that happens because of an action or set of conditions.

debate: An argument or discussion about an issue, generally between two sides.

expert: Someone who has a special skill or knowledge.

focus: Directed attention. Also, to direct attention or effort at something.

mental: Relating to the mind.

muscle: A part of the body that produces motion.

obesity: The condition of being very overweight.

organized: Set up in a formal way with rules for doing things.

physical: Relating to the body.

punishment: The act of making someone suffer for doing something wrong.

For More INFORMATION

WEBSITES

"It's Time to Play!"
kidshealth.org/en/kids/what-time.html
This article from the KidsHealth website features tips for being active and having fun in different kinds of weather and with different groups of people.

Try This: Fun Recess Games
fit.webmd.com/kids/move/article/recess-games
This website gives visitors ideas for new games to play during recess.

BOOKS

Bailey, Megan. *Fit and Fun.* Mankato, MN: The Child's World, 2014.

Balcom, Katherine. *Schoolyard.* New York, NY: AV2 by Weigl, 2015.

Miller, Connie Colwell. *You Can Handle Conflict: Hands or Words?* Mankato, MN: Amicus Publishing, 2018.

Publisher's note to educators and parents: Our editors have carefully reviewed these websites to ensure that they are suitable for students. Many websites change frequently, however, and we cannot guarantee that a site's future contents will continue to meet our high standards of quality and educational value. Be advised that students should be closely supervised whenever they access the Internet.

INDEX